The Likeable Expert

Blue Penguin Development, Inc.
One Ash Street
Hopkinton, MA 01748 USA
508-497-0900

Email: me@michaelkatz.com

Cover design: Mark Tatro

Back cover photo: Jonathan Katz

www.BluePenguinDevelopment.com

Copyright © 2017 Michael J. Katz
All rights reserved.
ISBN: 1975606663
ISBN-13: 978-1975606664

The Likeable Expert

121 Insights to Start Your Day and Grow Your Business

Michael J. Katz

2017

IV

The Likeable Expert

VI

For Evan, Emily, and Jonathan

Special thanks to:

… Belinda Wasser (aka RocketGirl), my friend and colleague, who keeps my business humming.

… Betsy Harper, my "water cooler" pal and fellow ice cream lover, who keeps me laughing every day.

… Nick Miller, my model for thinking big, who said "Yes" before I had even finished asking him to write the foreword of this book.

… Barry Shuchter, my genius tech resource, who doesn't mind my asking the same questions over and over again.

… Mark Levy, my brother from another mother, who is always eager to weigh in at a moment's notice.

… David Katz and Alan Katz, my brothers from the same mother, who have known me the longest.

And, most of all, my wife Linda, who never stops cheering for me.

x

Foreword

WHY YOU SHOULD READ THIS BOOK

"What a difference a day makes. Twenty-four little hours." The opening lines from Maria Grever's classic popular song, never more true than in Michael Katz's capable hands.

Each of us, independent professionals and solo practitioners, is pulled in multiple directions during most of those twenty-four little hours.

The trick is, every day, do one thing better. One thing that saves a little more time. One thing that boosts our satisfaction with the path we've chosen.

And that's the point of Michael's book, "TODAY, I . . . . ", this volume of "near daily, behind the scenes advice for busy professionals."

Michael is an experienced (and long-standing) independent professional whose powers of observation and expression stand beak and head above other penguins. Whether it's advice about a time saving app, a caution about choosing new clients, or a simple reminder to stay connected with our families and friends while we pursue our passions,

Michael's counsel almost always prompts the thoughts, "that's a really good idea" or, "thanks for the reminder, I've been meaning to get to that."

Each hint is short, a few moments to read. Implementation takes a little longer. Read them, one at a time. Savor them. Digest them. Take them to heart. Because that's the spot from which Michael wrote them.

Nick Miller
Founder and President
Clarity Advantage

Introduction

This book began life as a series of group emails—emails that I sent a few times a week to a dozen students in my one-year marketing course. The idea was to share some of the things I was doing "behind the scenes" to advance my own business.

Each email I sent began with the same phrase: "TODAY, I . . . "

People liked it. So I kept doing it, each time pointing out a small thing I had done that day.

Pretty soon I turned it into a public blog. Pretty soon after that (actually, a couple of years) I realized I had written and published over 350 of these.

This book (with some edits) is a compilation of what I consider to be the 121 best. I hope you find them useful in starting your day and growing your business.

Michael Katz
Hopkinton, Massachusetts
August 21, 2017

What is a Likeable Expert?

I didn't start out knowing anything about marketing a professional service business. In fact, I never intended to work for myself at all.

I went to college, I got an MBA, and I began working for other people. All perfectly fine . . . for a while, but after fifteen years, I became bored and tired of the same old routine. So, in 2000, I decided to go off on my own and become a consultant.

I ran into big problems almost immediately.

What I found was that while being smart, attentive, experienced, and all the rest were important, if only a few people have ever heard of you—and even fewer know, like, and trust you—you're going to have a hard time generating the business and income you want.

The Likeable Expert Advantage . . .

Eventually, I figured out that getting hired as a professional service provider (e.g., consultant, coach, recruiter, financial planner) requires three things:

1. People need to believe you are capable. They need to see you as an expert.

2. People need to like you. They need to trust you, feel comfortable with you, and value your point of view and perspective.

3. People need to remember you. You need to stay top of mind over time so that they think of you first when a problem arises.

In short, you need to be known as a Likeable Expert. This book, in bite-sized pieces, is a guide to getting you there.

TODAY, I . . .

The Likeable Expert

TODAY, I . . . have a new office chair.

Well, that's not exactly true.

What I have are the *pieces* of a new office chair, waiting to be assembled. It's all there. It's just not of any use to me yet.

Information works the same way. Thanks to Google, there's no shortage of it. The hard part is making sense of it.

Which is why when you write a newsletter or record a podcast or give a presentation to a group of businesspeople, you, too, want to focus on offering insight, not just piling on more information.

I'll be standing by in my office (literally) if you need me.

Michael J. Katz

TODAY, I . . . am waiting to hear back from a prospective client.

I sent them a couple of follow-up questions in an email last Friday, following a live conversation. Here it is Tuesday afternoon, and I'm still waiting.

They don't realize it, but I'm testing them to see how responsive they are. With every hour that passes, my interest in working with them drops a little bit more.

Isn't that backwards? Aren't clients supposed to test *us*, to see how quickly we get back to them?

Sure, but it cuts both ways.

Great clients, and not to be too cliché, treat you the way they'd like to be treated.

The ones who don't are usually trouble.

The Likeable Expert

TODAY, I . . . published a client's newsletter.

We published her company's first in March 2004.

Not only does working with the same client for more than a decade practically guarantee that things go smoothly, it also provides me with a steady and predictable source of income.

The second most important question to ask in deciding whether or not to work with a new client: "Is there an opportunity here for repeat business?"

(The most important: "Do I like these people?")

Michael J. Katz

TODAY, I . . . received an email from my bank.

The "from" field was: alerts

No bank name, no person's name . . . just the word "alerts" (it wasn't even capitalized).

Inside the email it began with: Dear ,

Were I The Invisible Man, this might be an appropriate greeting.

Of course, maybe my bank, the place with more of my personal information on file than pretty much any other institution on earth, doesn't know my first name.

The point is, if you're unsure what constitutes "good form" in email, social media, or whatever, hire somebody who knows. Looking like an amateur in one area carries over to the way others view you overall.

The Likeable Expert

TODAY, I . . . received a nice email from a long ago contact.

It was in response to a birthday card I sent her last week.

I send birthday cards to anyone who wants one (send me your snail mail address and date and I'll send you one too).

It's such an easy way to stay connected. It costs practically nothing.

But people always appreciate them.

Relationship marketing doesn't have to be a big deal, and it doesn't have to be expensive.

All you need is an idea, a plan, and a willingness to keep at it.

Michael J. Katz

TODAY, I . . . am creating a new webinar.

What's it called? Not really sure.

What's it about? Something to do with promoting and sharing the content you develop in broader, more systematic ways.

When will it be finished? Never.

Which is why I don't intend to wait until it's done and perfect to launch it. Because if I do, you'll never see it.

Webinars, web sites, newsletters, blogs, special reports, whatever.

The danger isn't in launching something before it's ready. It's in never launching something at all.

The Likeable Expert

TODAY, I . . . suggested a wording change.

A client shared his newsletter draft with me. It was a great article—interesting, topical, well written.

It ended with this sentence:

"Companies need to understand the importance of staying close to their customers."

I suggested he modify it to this instead:

"What are you doing to stay close to your customers?"

Same idea, more or less. But I think you'd agree that by asking a direct question, the latter feels way more engaging.

What are you doing to connect with your readers?

(See what I mean.)

Michael J. Katz

TODAY, I . . . had a good idea for a future newsletter.

I was backing out of a parking spot at the bank when it hit me.

So simple, I thought. There's no way I could forget that terrific insight.

But now, two hours later, I can't remember it.

Take my advice (but ignore my example), and write down the good ones as soon as you get them!

The Likeable Expert

TODAY, I . . . didn't give up.

I find it easy to stop working when it looks like a particular idea or project isn't going to be successful.

And so even before I know the answer, I'm inclined to (and often do) pull the plug and shift my focus to something else.

One of my plans for the coming year is to stop anticipating the result and instead just see what happens.

Michael J. Katz

TODAY, I . . . sent out a "last chance" reminder for a webinar I am presenting tomorrow.

I used to be very concerned with the question "How much do I promote this thing?" I didn't want to annoy people.

But somewhere along the way, I switched from thinking of it as "promoting" to "helping."

If you believe that the things you offer are valuable, you're doing people a disservice by not letting them know.

My email this morning will result in two things:

Some people will thank me for the reminder and sign up for tomorrow's webinar.

Some people will unsubscribe from my list entirely.

Which group do you think is more important to me?

The Likeable Expert

TODAY, I . . . stated a fee to a prospective client.

His response was, "That's a stretch, but I think we can do it."

To me, that's exactly what you're looking for: Near the top of what a prospect is willing to pay, but not over the line.

Of course, it's hard to know where that line is.

But I look at it this way: If nobody ever walks away from you on the basis of price, you're probably not charging enough.

Michael J. Katz

TODAY, I . . . spoke to two real estate attorneys.

We're getting ready to sell our house next spring.

Both attorneys came highly recommended and I'm sure both are well capable of handling our simple transaction.

The first talked and talked. Lots of detail about the process and why she was qualified. By the time she was done, I was more confused than when we began.

The second mostly asked questions. When he was out of things to ask, he described the process to me in about thirty seconds.

Who do you think we'll be hiring?

In a world where everybody is over the bar, people don't buy what you know. They buy who you are.

The Likeable Expert

TODAY, I . . . received a chilly email.

It came from someone who had invited me to partner on a potential project.

The project was kind of interesting but not quite right.

So I thanked him for the opportunity but politely declined.

His email back to me was very different in tone from the first one he sent. Not friendly, even a little bit angry.

The way somebody responds to "no" tells you a lot more about them than the way they respond to "yes."

Michael J. Katz

TODAY, I . . . received a very short email from a company promoting an upcoming event.

There were just fifty words in it. Two of them were misspelled.

And I don't mean "your vs. you're" type of misspelling, either.

"Future" was spelled "Tuture."

"Develop" was spelled "Develope."

We all make mistakes, but if your not even bothering to spell-check, your playing fast and loose with your hard-earned reputation as a Likeable Expert.

(P.S. The typos in the previous sentence were intentional.)

The Likeable Expert

TODAY, I . . . drove thirty minutes for a meeting.

It was with someone whose company might be a good partner for me.

He initially suggested a "phone meeting."

I said I didn't mind. I'd be happy to come to him.

So I drove there. And shook his hand. And sat in his office. And gave him a copy of my book when I left.

Virtual is great. But when it's possible and you want to make a strong connection, nothing beats face-to-face (even with my face).

Michael J. Katz

TODAY, I . . . am helping a new client prepare for their newsletter launch.

The office manager keeps asking me about the rules I have in place:

"What's the deadline for sending you new names to be added to the list?"

"How much lead time do you need between when we sign off on final copy and when we publish?"

"What format do edits need to be in?"

My answer, whenever possible, is "I don't have a lot of rules—whatever works best for you."

Could I establish more formal procedures? Sure. And if I were a bigger company, I'd have to. But one of the advantages of being super-small is that you can usually be super-accommodating too.

(Clients really like that.)

The Likeable Expert

TODAY, I . . . got some really good advice.

It was from my friend Mark, who told me—after I called him up and asked for suggestions—that the title of this book is wrong.

He thinks it should have been called: *Today, I . . .*

Mark knows a lot about book publishing. He's a fantastic writer. He understands what sells and what doesn't. He cares whether or not I'm successful.

And I almost changed it because I'm sure he's right.

But . . . even though his suggestions make sense, I'm just way more excited about calling it *The Likeable Expert*.

And so I did.

Sometimes you just have to go with what feels best.

Michael J. Katz

TODAY, I . . . listened to an election-related anecdote on the radio.

You know . . . the kind where they interview some random person who has had an experience that supports the position of one of the candidates.

The anecdotes are offered as evidence.

Of course, they are nothing of the sort. One person's experience (or even those of one thousand persons) in a country of 320 million is beyond immaterial.

You may as well trot out somebody who was bitten by a runaway lobster in the supermarket and claim that it's indicative of "a growing trend of rogue lobster attacks."

Yet it's very persuasive. Because we like and understand stories a whole lot more than we like and understand statistics.

The Likeable Expert

If you're relying on statistics at the expense of stories in your marketing, you'll find it equally hard to persuade prospective lobsters. I mean clients.

Michael J. Katz

TODAY, I . . . met with a prospective email newsletter client.

Last week, while finalizing meeting details, I sent him a two-page report I'd written called, "The 5 Biggest Blocks to Writing a Monthly Newsletter (and how to overcome them right away)."

In the email, I said, "I thought you might find the attached short article useful."

Today when we met, he had it printed out and sitting on the conference room table in front of him.

You can wait until you arrive at the meeting to start the sales process.

Or (recommended), you can pique the interest of a prospect and start the ball rolling before the "official" conversation even begins.

The Likeable Expert

TODAY, I . . . am celebrating my 27th wedding anniversary.

The thing is, it doesn't feel like Linda and I have been married for 27 years—it feels more like 9,855 *days*.

None of the individual days matter in particular. I can't even remember most of them. But when you put them all together, it adds up to something big.

Relationship marketing works the same way. There's no single thing you're going to say or do that will make your business well known and successful.

There's no meeting you attend or individual newsletter you write or client you help that will instantly change everything.

It's only over time that all the little things you do add up to something big.

Michael J. Katz

TODAY, I . . . bought some paint.

When my wife and I were at Lowe's over the weekend, the guy at the paint desk was wonderfully knowledgeable and helpful.

In a matter of just a few minutes, he helped us narrow down the best options available for painting our deck.

Today, when I returned to buy the paint, there was a different guy at the paint desk. He knew next to nothing about paint and seemed miffed that I had interrupted his time staring blankly off into space.

This is one of our HUGE advantages as solos and small-business owners.

Once a company has more than even a handful of people on staff, it's very hard to provide a consistent level of service and style of communication.

For us, it's easy . . . provided we pay attention to how we connect with the outside world!

The Likeable Expert

TODAY, I . . . started my snow blower.

Not because I expect snow. Rather, because the guy who I use to service my snow blower has a special offer:

"Schedule a tune-up in the next thirty days and get a discounted rate."

I started it to make sure it would. If it didn't, I would have made a service appointment.

What I like about this guy's approach is that he's found a way to (somewhat) smooth the peaks and valleys of his service business, something whose "product" can't be inventoried.

What can you do to accomplish the same?

Michael J. Katz

TODAY, I . . . received an email from my accountant.

I had sent her a quick question about an hour before.

She said, "Such a coincidence! I just finished reading your latest newsletter!"

To tell you the truth, I'm kind of surprised she even reads it.

But who knows? Maybe she was having a slow day; maybe she just needed a quick break; maybe the subject line caught her eye.

Whatever it was, publishing regularly keeps me top of mind with a wide range of people, most of whom are not—and never will be—clients.

Some of those people mention me to others; some of those others hire me.

Publishing regularly is marketing magic!

The Likeable Expert

TODAY, I . . . received a call from somebody looking for "Ralph."

I said, "Sorry, you have the wrong number."

She said, "Oh, well, maybe you can help me. This is Darlene. I'm calling on behalf of . . ."

And she was off and running (until . . . it's possible I hung up on her).

If your first bit of outreach to a potential client is to trick them, you're not going to build much of a business.

Michael J. Katz

TODAY, I . . . closed the door on a prospective client.

Jim and I had a nice conversation about a newsletter for his law firm when he called a few weeks ago.

I sent a follow-up email right afterward.

And another one a week later.

And one more after that.

No response to any of them!

So today I sent an email wishing him all the best and saying that I assumed he had "moved on to other things."

You can hang on forever chasing phantom prospects, or you can take control and close the door yourself.

I find the former to be an energy killer and the latter to be exactly the opposite!

The Likeable Expert

TODAY, I . . . received a gift from Michelle.

Michelle was a student in my marketing course last year.

She sent me a very nice package of fruit (and other tasty treats!) as thanks for my sending her a referral who turned into a client.

I bet "word of mouth" is the primary way you find new clients too.

Do you have a "thank you process" in place—as Michelle apparently does—to make sure there are more mouths involved on your behalf?

Michael J. Katz

TODAY, I . . . received an email from a friend.

She was lamenting the slow and uneven growth of her business.

I said, "Great, that's the way it generally happens."

The video that goes viral, the best-selling book, the business that makes one small tweak and explodes on the scene . . . they are all exceptions. Winning lottery tickets.

Unfortunately, we've become conditioned to believe that's the norm. And if we don't "achieve" that, we must be doing something wrong.

Slow and steady is the way it works. The only mistake is to stop moving forward.

The Likeable Expert

TODAY, I . . . heard the accountant in the office across the hall talking to the UPS man.

They were having a laugh about how crazy tax season was. The accountant said how glad he was to be through it.

Working like crazy in Q1 is part of the culture of that profession.

Do you have to go along with it? Well, just yesterday I spoke with another accountant who told me that he's worked out an approach so that he never has to.

Are you doing things because you have to or just because that's what everyone else does?

Michael J. Katz

TODAY, I . . . spoke with somebody about maybe hiring him.

When it came to his fee, he was very "squishy."

Lots of hesitation, lots of ums and ahs.

Before I could say anything, he said he might be able to drop it down a bit.

If you don't believe in your own value—and the fees you charge—nobody else will either.

(Hint: Practice saying it out loud in front of the mirror until it sounds reasonable to you!)

The Likeable Expert

TODAY, I . . . rewrote parts of my web site.

Of course, that's not big news. I fiddle with it about once a week.

Tweaking words, phrases, and sometimes entire pages.

I doubt you change yours as frequently, but the concept still applies: Your web site needs to feel fresh and represent you, your work, and your point of view accurately.

If the last time you updated yours was midway through the Clinton administration, it's time to take another look.

Michael J. Katz

TODAY, I . . . received a request to edit something I wrote.

It came from a popular blog that is publishing one of my articles.

They want to remove the second sentence (below) because it's "too negative."

"Now, I don't mean to suggest that my dog, Abbie, is smarter than you. Nor am I implying that you have anything but a modest and appropriate interest in horse manure (you do subscribe to this newsletter, after all)."

Many people (and companies) are deathly afraid of saying anything that might be taken the wrong way, diminish the brand, raise an eyebrow.

And then, once the content they've created is appropriately plain vanilla-ized, they try to figure out why they're having so much trouble standing out from the pack.

The Likeable Expert

TODAY, I . . . have accomplished nothing.

I never do on Monday mornings. I've learned that it takes me a while to get started productively each week, so I avoid scheduling anything important.

This afternoon, when I'll be a little tired, I'll work on a writing project that requires me to be funny. I've learned that the quirky humor flows more easily then.

You can force yourself to do certain things at certain times. Or you can be aware of your own cycles and schedule the work that fits.

Michael J. Katz

TODAY, I . . . heard from a friend who was laid off last week.

It seems like it's happening more and more, especially to people in the 50+ age group.

It's also a good reminder that when you own your own business, as difficult and scary as some days may be, you're the one who writes the rules.

If you're working for yourself, you're already successful.

The Likeable Expert

TODAY, I . . . told a potential client that I wasn't a good match.

Nice people, but the kind of content development they were looking for wasn't quite within the range of what I want to do (or, frankly, what I'm particularly good at).

"Bad" clients and projects don't just happen. The best way to avoid them is to never get started in the first place.

Michael J. Katz

TODAY, I . . . launched something early.

It's a six-month group coaching class that begins in a month.

"Early" because it will be a scramble to get all the promotional elements and class materials ready in time.

It would definitely be easier to just put it off for a couple of months until it is more perfect.

What I've discovered, though, is that launching good things—whether that's a newsletter, a business, a class, or something else—is much better than *not* launching perfect things.

The Likeable Expert

TODAY, I . . . told a prospect I could probably help her.

It wasn't that long ago that I would have said "definitely" right off the bat and then done my best to convince her of why (even if it wasn't entirely true).

I was focused on closing rather than helping.

Not only does my newer approach lead to fewer disappointments (for both of us), it also turns out to be a pretty good way of demonstrating trustworthiness.

Michael J. Katz

TODAY, I . . . responded to people who "liked" an article I posted on LinkedIn.

Not to all of them, but to those I had either lost touch with or wanted to stay connected to.

I'm big on publishing content . . . but don't stop there.

The people who respond to things we create are worth staying close to.

The Likeable Expert

TODAY, I . . . asked for a 50% deposit from a new client.

They were under a deadline and weren't sure how fast they could cut a check.

I said, "No problem. I'll be here when you're ready." An hour later, they called with a credit card number.

Two important things:

1. Always get a deposit and a signed agreement from a new client. Don't worry. The people who are for real are never insulted when you ask for that.

2. Don't let somebody else's urgency become your problem.

Michael J. Katz

TODAY, I . . . received an email from my graphic designer.

He told me that he was raising his rates, but . . .

. . . because I "am so good to him" with the referrals I send and my own work, I am locked in at the old rate forever.

Things to think about:

Do you think I will continue to be "good to him" as a result?

Do you think I am more or less likely to consider using another designer in the future?

Do you think he just did something really smart?

The Likeable Expert

TODAY, I . . . got to my office at 10 a.m.

Actually, I get here every day at about 10 a.m.

And I usually go home around six.

It took me a long time to realize that I get to set my own work hours. (It took me even longer to realize that my company has no dress code.)

What "rules" are you still following?

Michael J. Katz

TODAY, I . . . picked up a *Sports Illustrated* while waiting in the doctor's office.

I wasn't reading closely, just kind of flipping through the pages, looking at the pictures and the captions.

The stories and athletes were all current, but something didn't feel quite right.

When I got to a "coloring page," I realized that I had picked up *Sports Illustrated for Kids.*

Same subject, different audience . . . totally different presentation.

If you're not thinking about your audience when you create content, don't be surprised if you strike out (sorry).

The Likeable Expert

TODAY, I . . . spoke to a prospective client.

Along the way and after she told me a bit about what she was looking for, I asked her my favorite prospective client question:

"Why don't you just do this yourself?"

(In other words, why does this person believe that he/she needs outside help?)

She responded the way nearly everybody does: "Good question." Then she went on to explain.

Your best question may be different.

Either way, it took me a long time to realize that asking good questions is the key to effective selling.

What's *your* best question?

Michael J. Katz

TODAY, I . . . sent a thank you note.

It was to the woman who runs the ice cream stand where I held my company birthday party last week.

No big deal . . . just a few words of thanks and a "see you next year!"

I send one hand-written snail mail note a week.

That's fifty opportunities a year to connect with people in my network in a strong and memorable way.

Of course, it's pretty difficult to do: You need a piece of paper, a pen, an envelope, and a stamp. And five entire minutes.

I guess that's why most people don't bother.

The Likeable Expert

TODAY, I . . . received a letter in the mail from a bookkeeper.

Inside: A full color, six-panel brochure; a high-quality business card; a hand-written, customized envelope.

I'd give this approach an A+ . . . if it were 1995.

Today, though, it's largely a waste of money.

Given that the cost of staying in touch with people you already know is zero, snail mail campaigns to strangers are both more expensive and less productive than simply finding ways to have an ongoing conversation with your existing relationships.

Michael J. Katz

TODAY, I . . . received a newsletter.

The subject line was: August 2017 Newsletter from (Company Name).

I'm pretty sure I can guess what next month's subject line will be.

Your subject line is a headline.

And while the content within is what's most important, if nobody opens your email, it doesn't really matter.

The Likeable Expert

TODAY, I . . . am preparing for a full-day, private workshop I'm giving in Toronto this week.

I asked the conference organizer for a list of session attendees so that I could send a preliminary email to them asking what they hoped to learn in our session.

This has two benefits:

First, it helps me know, going in, the topics that people are most interested in.

Second, it allows me to extend the length of our "conversation" beyond just the day of the workshop. That's why I'll also send a follow-up email to the group after the session.

The more opportunities you can create to interact, the more likely you are to make a lasting connection.

Michael J. Katz

TODAY, I . . . received a question by email.

It was from someone who had just completed my (outstanding) email newsletter home study course.

She was excited about building a business in which she would create newsletters for other companies.

I asked her what her own newsletter was about. It turns out she doesn't have one.

Uh oh. If you don't believe in what you're doing, why would I hire you to do it for me?

The Likeable Expert

TODAY, I . . . read an email from August 2015.

It had a link to an article that had been sitting in my inbox since then. I finally clicked and read it.

Email is a long way from "permanent."

But it's an equally long way from the "here and it's gone" nature of social media. The links within those are still out there, but I can't imagine ever going back months (let alone years) into my Twitter or LinkedIn or Facebook feed to find something.

If you're not regularly using email in your marketing, you're missing out on a zero-cost means of reaching the people you want to reach.

Michael J. Katz

TODAY, I . . . gave somebody his deposit back.

It was a small writing project, but the further along we went, the clearer it became that we were not a good match.

I suppose I could have just soldiered on, but why?

It was an arduous process for me, and I doubt he would have been thrilled with the result no matter how much time we spent.

Clients can pull the plug if they no longer want to work with you.

Shouldn't you have the same option?

The Likeable Expert

TODAY, I . . . received an email from my friend Robert.

Somebody unsubscribed from his newsletter because they thought his subject line was, to paraphrase, "inappropriate."

I congratulated him.

Partly because I had emailed him earlier in the day to say that I thought that same subject line was brilliant.

But also because it's a fine example of a marketing truth: You can't get people to love you without risking the possibility that others will hate you.

Of course, you could just play it safe and publish the same old boring "industry best practices" sediment in the same old boring way. I've heard that's a surefire way to stand out from the crowd too.

Michael J. Katz

TODAY, I . . . am six weeks into testing a new idea.

I've got about seventy-five people helping me trial it.

I don't know where it's headed.

I don't know what the level of interest will be.

I have no idea how much revenue it may generate (if any).

I am literally making it up as I go along.

I sure am enjoying it.

If you need to know the ending before you begin, you're not going to have many beginnings.

The Likeable Expert

TODAY, I . . . didn't sign a contract.

It was a simple thing in connection with a (nearly) free talk I was invited to give.

But they wanted me to sign an agreement, something I don't do, ever, without my attorney first reviewing.

Given the small fee, it's not worth my getting her involved.

Having rules of engagement for your business that you've developed ahead of time streamlines decisions down the road.

Michael J. Katz

TODAY, I . . . had someone thank me.

For a presentation I gave in person earlier this week that she heard much of as part of a previous presentation a couple of years ago.

She told me how happy she was for the reminder.

Repetition is how we learn. Worry less about repeating yourself and more about being consistent.

The Likeable Expert

TODAY, I . . . "wasted" two hours in the middle of the day.

I walked my dog in the woods and then took a nap on the couch.

But then I got back to my computer and banged out three things in a row, with better results than if I had pushed through earlier in the day when I didn't feel like it.

Following your own rhythm is both more productive and more enjoyable.

Michael J. Katz

TODAY, I . . . made a list of thirteen things that I intend to do this week.

I make a list like this every Monday morning, crossing things off as the week goes by.

If you want to feel (and be) productive, keep the list short—but get it done.

The Likeable Expert

TODAY, I . . . received a new sign-up for my newsletter.

In the field labelled "How did you learn of this newsletter," she typed the name of somebody I had lost touch with up until a few days ago, when I emailed him just to say hello.

Coincidence?

Or do you think my "hello email," which contained exactly zero self promotion by the way, is what prompted my long-lost friend to share my name with somebody else?

You don't need to sell yourself at every turn to succeed . . . but you do need to be consistently visible.

Who can you reconnect with today?

Michael J. Katz

TODAY, I . . . was asked by a prospect, "Why should I hire you?"

I said, "I'm not sure you should. In fact, I think we are about 70% right for each other."

Two things happened as a result.

First, it broke the ice. Up until then we had been having a pretty formal, prospect-consultant back and forth. She was expecting me to "pitch" her and was taken by surprise when I went in the other direction.

Second, we moved on to a frank, authentic discussion. Once she realized I wasn't trying to convince her of anything, we worked together to see if we were a good match.

We weren't. I referred her to somebody more appropriate and wished her well.

Did she hire me? No. But one day in the future, somebody she sends my way—as a result of today's interaction—will.

The Likeable Expert

TODAY, I . . . offered a discount.

I offered a half-off price on one product to those who had previously purchased something else.

People who've purchased from / hired you in the past are way (as in WAY) more likely than a non-buyer to buy from you again in the future.

These are your peeps!

Are you rolling out the red carpet for these people, or are you just throwing them back in the pile with everyone else?

Michael J. Katz

TODAY, I . . . suggested that a client purchase a domain name (URL).

The domain I suggested was her own name.

When you own your own name (e.g., www.michaelkatz.com), it's a nice shortcut for telling people how to find you (especially if your "official" web site URL is not so easy to remember).

Depending on how common your name is, it may no longer be available (note to Joe Smith; don't bother looking). But, yours may still be out there.

Check availability here: www.betterwhois.com

P.S. You can point as many domains to the same web site as you like, so there's no conflict in having your own name and your official company name point to the same place, as mine does.

The Likeable Expert

TODAY, I . . . woke up early.

Then I exercised for an hour.

Then I had breakfast, in the morning sun, on the back deck.

I do pretty much the same thing every day.

If your goal as a solo professional is "to become successful," you might be overlooking what you've already achieved.

Michael J. Katz

TODAY, I . . . received an email from Cindy.

She shared this with me:

I went out for lunch with the Global VP of Customer Experience for [FORTUNE 500 COMPANY] last week and sent him a thank you card afterward. He sent me this:

Hi, Cindy,

Can't remember the last time I received a hand-written card with an actual postage stamp (bills don't count).
Thanks.

/Dave

But if snail mail is so good, won't the channel fill up until we're all barraged with handwritten notes? Sure, right after your gym fills up with all the people exercising every day.

Don't worry. If there's effort and/or cost involved, there's never a line.

TODAY, I . . . updated my email signature to reflect a change in my business focus.

And my LinkedIn profile.

And my web site header.

And my "services" page.

And my bio.

And everywhere else I could think of.

Consistency is at the heart of word of mouth (assuming your mouth has a heart). When you make a move, try to get everything pointed in the same direction!

Michael J. Katz

TODAY, I . . . read an article about robots.

It was from *Inc.* magazine—an interview with a guy whose company is attempting to automate farming and gardening.

Here's one thing he said regarding his "laws of robotics":

"First, too many robots are created with multiple features so that they can be deployed in multiple situations. Those general-use robots can do lots of things but excel at none."

Replace "robots" with "professionals" and you've got a pretty good description of the way most people market themselves.

Are you narrow enough in focus to excel at something in particular?

The Likeable Expert

TODAY, I . . . repeated myself.

I explained something to a prospective client using a string of sentences that I've said (at least) a hundred times before to other people.

That's the way it's supposed to work.

When it comes to describing what you do, the idea is to keep fine-tuning it, until it's the best possible presentation of that idea that you can manage.

If you don't feel like a broken record, you're not doing it right (I've probably said that to you before).

Michael J. Katz

TODAY, I . . . just realized that my shirt is on inside out.

And it's 2:45 p.m.

I don't know if I'm more troubled by the fact that I didn't notice, or that I spent an hour with my wife at lunch and *she* didn't notice.

Either way, it's a good reminder that it's easy to overlook things you see every day.

When was the last time you took a focused walk through your own web site?

The Likeable Expert

TODAY, I . . . am unhappy with Budget Rent A Car.

Actually, I passed "unhappy" about five miles back. I am bouncing-off-the-wall angry.

Rude, inept, a tangle of "not our policy" bureaucratic blah blah.

But it's understandable. It's really hard to treat people like people when you're running a factory. There's just no time or energy or room for it.

A good reminder that as we scale our respective businesses we need to make sure that we never get anywhere near that line.

Michael J. Katz

TODAY, I . . . read a quote by Joseph Campbell.

"If you do follow your bliss you put yourself on a kind of track that has been there all the while, waiting for you."

Pretty fluffy stuff—the kind of thing I never would have shared back when I had a job and was trying to "look professional."

Maybe that's why I left.

Maybe Joseph Campbell knew something that most people don't.

The Likeable Expert

TODAY, I . . . am waiting to hear back from my tech guy.

He used to respond within hours. Now it might be a day (or two).

Not long ago I encouraged him to raise his rates (a lot).

Now he's really, really busy.

Hmm . . . do you think there's a connection?

Michael J. Katz

TODAY, I . . . received an email from a prospective client.

Two sentences, all business, asking about my interest in a particular project.

When I responded and noticing that the writer lived in Seattle, I mentioned that my daughter, Emily, lives in nearby Tacoma (aka, "How far can I get from my parents without actually leaving the continental United States?").

His email back to me a couple of hours later was considerably warmer and even included mention of a camping trip he is taking with his own daughter this weekend.

It may seem that business is just about business. But if you can find ways to make connections on a human level, too, you're bound to have a whole lot more of it.

The Likeable Expert

TODAY, I . . . heard from a client.

Last week I sent him a joke gift.

I was on a group call with him when someone happened to mention Helen Reddy (long story).

We all had such a big laugh about it that after we hung up I sent him one of her albums.

Today, he called and left me a 60-second message, at least half of which was him laughing.

No reason you can't have fun while earning a living.

Michael J. Katz

TODAY, I . . . went to a networking meeting and had nice conversations with about five people.

Now I'm sitting in Starbucks sending individual emails to each of them saying it was nice to meet them (it was).

This follow-up part is at least as important as the networking meeting itself!

The Likeable Expert

TODAY, I . . . replied to a newsletter that I received.

I thought it was a good piece, so I clicked "reply" and complimented the sender.

She wrote right back to thank me.

We're all producing content—but it can seem as if few people are actually listening.

When you take a moment to let people know that you heard—and benefited from—something they said, you stand out from all the people who never bother.

Michael J. Katz

TODAY, I . . . read an email newsletter success story.

Sharon sent me the following:

"I just got an email from someone who got last week's email newsletter forwarded from a current client and she wants to talk."

The content you create—newsletter, video, blog, free download, etc.—is a tool that others can use to share you.

The more you create, the more opportunities that follow.

The Likeable Expert

TODAY, I . . . read a blog post that described in detail how to sell an online product.

At least half of what it recommends conflicts with a long article I read last week on the same topic.

Both articles were written by "experts."

Experts, even the most qualified ones, tell you *A* way to do something. But it's rarely the only way.

Learn what you can. Develop an approach that works for you. Stop second-guessing yourself.

Michael J. Katz

TODAY, I . . . got a visit from 1992.

It was a door-to-door saleswoman selling office supplies.

Driving around town, knocking on random doors, hoping to find a stranger who needs what she's selling at this precise moment. I can't imagine a less productive approach.

You know what the opposite of this is?

Sitting in your office, communicating regularly with people you know, who've asked to hear from you—and who will call you when the time is right.

If you don't have a house list that you talk with regularly, I sure hope you've got some pretty amazing office supplies.

The Likeable Expert

TODAY, I . . . listened to a salesman at my local coffee shop.

He wasn't talking to me; he was on the phone.

Apparently, and according to what I overheard, what makes his company different is "our experience" and "a strong commitment to customer service."

If the words you rely on to separate yourself from everyone else are the same words that everyone else uses, it's going to be a long selling day.

Michael J. Katz

TODAY, I . . . suggested to a client that we hold off on publishing her newsletter for an extra day.

There's a big snowstorm coming today and tomorrow, and her newsletter would normally go out Wednesday.

But Wednesday is a day when many people will be just getting back to work. They'll be in "catch up" mode and therefore eagerly deleting whatever is not urgent.

There are no best days and times to publish a newsletter. But there are *worst* days and times.

I try to avoid holidays, school vacation weeks, and major weather events!

The Likeable Expert

TODAY, I . . . helped someone simplify the way she describes her work.

She's an attorney in one of my classes, and we were working on a one sentence description of her niche.

If you're someone who's fond of precision and detail—lawyers, engineers, financial planners—this can be a difficult task. A one sentence description of anything meaningful will necessarily be an oversimplification.

But it's necessary in the word of mouth world we live in.

You have two options:

Option #1: Oversimplify.

Option #2: Tell me everything and be forgotten instantly.

Michael J. Katz

TODAY, I . . . went to the web site of someone whom I met the other day.

It was a well-designed site, and I was happy to see that he had a blog. A blog (and/or newsletter) is a great way for people to check you out and get a sense of what it would be like to work with you.

Uh oh. The most recent post was from November 2014.

The only thing worse than no content is old content.

Try to keep things up to date on your site (and take down that blog if you are not able to keep it current)!

The Likeable Expert

TODAY, I . . . asked someone, "What type of client is a perfect match for you?"

Loooong silence, followed by an even longer ramble of off the cuff blah blah.

When you can clearly and succinctly describe your perfect client, two good things happen:

Good thing number one: Prospects hear that, and if they fit what you're describing, feel confident knowing there's a match.

Good thing number two: Non-prospects (aka, all other humans) learn whom you're looking for and, when they come across those people, are more likely to send them your way.

Michael J. Katz

TODAY, I . . . received an email from someone who wanted to know about fees.

He saw a package described on my web site and sent a one sentence email asking what it cost.

I didn't answer the question.

Instead, I suggested we talk so that I could find out more about the kind of work he does and why/how he thinks he may need some help.

In my experience, the "good prospects" are eager for the opportunity to talk more. The "tire kickers," on the other hand—the people who are just shopping on price—rarely are.

Ignoring the "How much?" question in the beginning turns out to be a pretty good filter of who's worth spending time with.

The Likeable Expert

TODAY, I . . . received an enthusiastic thank you email from a client.

She was thanking me for the thank you note I sent her last week (still with me?).

I was thanking her for taking time to speak with someone I sent her way—another client who was looking for some information.

Three questions for you:

1. Do you think she would have responded the way she did if my note were an email rather than hand-written?

2. Do you think I helped my business by taking the time to thank her?

3. Can you think of someone to whom you could send a thank you note right now? (I know, that was kind of a trick question.)

Michael J. Katz

TODAY, I . . . went to the Registry of Motor Vehicles.

It's a cliché but well earned. And whether it's anybody's fault or not, it's filled with lessons for solos:

Unclear signage

Conflicting information

Uncomfortable seating

Poor communication

Condescension

No WiFi for crying out loud!

If you can't identify dozens of ways to outmaneuver your larger competitors, you're not paying enough attention.

The Likeable Expert

TODAY, I . . . am preparing for a webinar that I'm presenting tomorrow.

It will take me about an hour to get ready.

The first time I presented this webinar it took me about a week.

There is a lot of "value leverage" (assuming that's a term) in selling the same thing, multiple times, to different people.

That might be a product, a service, a technique, a package, a class, a webinar, or something else.

What can you resell?

Michael J. Katz

TODAY, I . . . listened to a company CEO talk on the radio.

No matter what he was asked, he spun the answer in a positive way:

Is Amazon hurting your market share?

"They're a part of the pie, certainly, but we are all growing."

Did changing strategy a couple of years ago hurt your profitability?

"It was a temporary hit, but we're headed in the right direction now and doing well."

I'm fairly certain that were he asked whether or not he found it painful to be run over by a drunken herd of oxen, he'd respond by describing it as "an important learning experience."

I don't blame the man. He's head of a large public company. He can't afford to give truly candid answers.

But you and I are not.

The Likeable Expert

Admitting what you don't know, or what didn't work, or what you're losing sleep over is not only a pretty good way to connect with other humans (who are often feeling the same way), because of that, it's also an effective marketing tactic that your larger competitors simply cannot match.

Michael J. Katz

TODAY, I . . . received eight chocolate bars in the mail.

They were sent to me by someone I partnered with on a recent project—kind of a "thank you and congrats to the two of us."

You know what I noticed?

Sending a thank you gift when a project is done—especially a gift so nice and unexpected—leaves the other person with a final, extremely positive feeling overall.

First impressions may matter. But it's the last experience you have with someone, good or bad, that's the longest lasting—and maybe, therefore, the most important one of all.

What's your "Client Congratulations" gift?

The Likeable Expert

TODAY, I . . . received a wonderful email note.

It was from someone who just finished one of my classes.

I thanked her and then did three things:

1. I asked her permission to "use your name and an excerpt of what you wrote" as a testimonial (she said "yes").

2. I posted her comment on the page that promotes the class.

3. I filed her email and associated permission in my "testimonials" folder. (In 17+ years I've never had a testimonial come back to bite me, but if you're going to use somebody's words and name, it's a good idea to keep a record of the permission!)

Receiving praise for your work feels great (I never tire of it).

But using it effectively is what brings more clients.

Michael J. Katz

TODAY, I . . . didn't send a promotional email to everyone on my list.

I sent an email today promoting a free webinar I'm offering next week. But I didn't send it to 223 people.

Why? Because they've opted out of receiving promotional emails (an option I provide within each promotional email I send).

By providing this choice, I can continue to talk to them without losing them entirely.

People appreciate having options. What can you do to offer more of them?

The Likeable Expert

TODAY, I . . . am rereading a book called *Do The Work!,* by Steven Pressfield.

There are a number of gems in this short book (98 pages).

Here's what he says regarding a screenplay he wrote that bombed as a movie:

"My friend Tony Keppelman snapped me out of it by asking if I was going to quit. Hell, no! 'Then be happy,' he said. 'You're where you wanted to be, aren't you? So you're taking a few blows. That's the price for being in the arena and not on the sidelines. Stop complaining and be grateful.'"

Here's to being in the arena.

Michael J. Katz

TODAY, I . . . got my lawnmower fixed.

I had been unable to remove the rusted bolt holding the blade despite whatever tools of mine (and my neighbors) I tried.

So I took it to a local gas station and asked the mechanic if he could help.

He loosened it in about fifteen seconds, wished me a nice day, and went smiling back inside.

Yesterday, that gas station was unremarkable to me, one of dozens within a five-mile radius from my house. Today, it looks completely different.

Sometimes, fifteen seconds helping a stranger is the best marketing you can do.

The Likeable Expert

TODAY, I . . . received a one sentence email from my friend Paul.

He asked:

"Michael—please tell me again the name of your client/associate who is a sales recruiter."

Betsy Harper (SMSearch.com) immediately popped into my head. I sent her contact info to Paul.

So, what super-simple, everyday question causes *you* to pop into someone's head?

(If you answered, "I don't know," maybe it's worth thinking about.)

Michael J. Katz

TODAY, I . . . am asking for help.

I'm sharing the "sales page" for my soon to be released product with a few dozen trusted friends and colleagues.

Nothing formal. I'm simply sending an email asking each of them to give it a look and let me know if they see any typos, broken links, or anything else that is obviously wrong.

That's not the way I used to do it. Instead, my inclination is to work on something until I think it's perfect and then introduce it with a big TA-DA!

But I've found that enlisting the help of other people before the cement is dry makes the eventual TA-DA go much more smoothly.

The Likeable Expert

TODAY, I . . . visited the web site of someone whose blog post I had stumbled upon.

He seemed very impressive.

Professionally designed site, plenty of content, brand name client list, lots of social media shares.

I noticed that he offered a one-hour consultation, so I gave it a look. It only cost $200.

Interestingly, my immediate next thought was not, "Wow, that's not much for a guy this well established."

Instead, it was, "Oh, maybe he's not that good."

Price is about more than just how much money you put into your pocket today. It's also data that people use, in part, to make judgments about you.

Is your low price helping you or hurting you?

Michael J. Katz

TODAY, I . . . spent ten minutes connecting with people on LinkedIn.

Not promoting my own work—just scrolling down my home page, seeing who got promoted or had a new photo or posted an interesting article.

Sometimes I congratulated someone. Sometimes I made a comment about a post. Sometimes I just said "Hey, nice to see you."

It's easy—and fun. And if you don't think that's marketing, you're working way too hard.

The Likeable Expert

TODAY, I . . . have been thinking about something.

How can I "corner the market" on what it is I do?

Not just a niche—something bigger, something more precise.

What can I know or create or be that makes me the *only* reasonable solution to a critical problem?

I think it's something worth thinking about.

Michael J. Katz

TODAY, I . . . gave someone a copy of my book.

We were having coffee, and it seemed like it would be useful to her, so I gave her one.

Free, useful, hardcopy content is a great tool to have at the ready as a giveaway, either in person or through the mail.

It doesn't have to be a book. A free report, an audio CD, an oversized postcard, a tablet you've carved, whatever.

Hardcopy, however, has a much bigger impact.

Does it cost a little money? Sure. That's why it has an impact. People appreciate the gesture.

Develop two or three (or more) free things you can give away when the moment is right.

TODAY, I . . . made $2,500 in one hour.

I delivered a webinar: 25 people X $100 each = $2,500.00

Of course, that's not really true. If you add up all the prep time and overhead, I probably earned $30 an hour.

So is it worth it? Not if you only do it once.

Whether developing a book, CD, course, system, approach, webinar, or any other new project, most of the cost is in the first one.

Most of the profit comes from doing/selling it over and over again.

Michael J. Katz

TODAY, I . . . am preparing for a talk I'm giving at a trade show next week.

So I just updated and printed my introduction. Double-spaced.

That day I'll hand it to whoever is introducing me.

He or she may already have something and already be prepared.

But just as likely, they're walking in cold with the intention of winging it.

When you hand them the introduction, they read it out loud, word for word, every time.

The Likeable Expert

TODAY, I . . . read an article about making your blog standout.

You know, the usual tips about "rising to the top," "developing thousands of passionate followers," "becoming a blogging superstar."

Not that you asked, but I think it's garbage.

There's just not enough room for more than a few people at the top, whatever your industry. Most of us will never get anywhere close.

Which is why my publishing strategy—my marketing strategy—is to game the system: I focus my thought and energy on the people I already know.

I don't need to be at the top of Google. I just need to be visible, valued and liked by the very small group of people on earth who already know me.

When you view the world through the lens of relationship, there's not much competition at all.

Michael J. Katz

TODAY, I . . . was invited by a client to their "holiday open house."

There was a time when I thought of clients as my "bosses"—people I worked for on a contract basis.

Now I think of them as colleagues, partners, and often friends . . . people I work *with*.

Not only does this change in perspective lead to better, higher paying work, it makes for a nicer experience all around.

The best clients recognize that they need you as much as you need them. And they treat you that way.

(Hint: Lose the ones who don't.)

The Likeable Expert

TODAY, I . . . asked the guy who serviced my lawn mower:

"Is it better to empty all the gas when I put the mower away for the winter or fill it to the top?"

I bet he's heard that question before.

In fact, I bet for every fifty "What's your opinion on this?" questions he gets regarding small engine repair/service, he's heard forty-nine of them before.

I bet you hear the same questions over and over again regarding your profession too.

Guess what? Those common questions—the ones you hear all the time from your target clients—are the things you should be writing and talking about.

Simple insights are what the "outsiders" crave.

Michael J. Katz

TODAY, I . . . called someone back who had left me a message.

I knew from her voice mail that what she wanted wasn't part of the services I offer.

But I called her anyway to tell her that and to suggest someone else who could help.

The best opportunities for building your reputation as a likeable expert are those in which there's absolutely no benefit to you. (Today.)

The Likeable Expert

TODAY, I . . . sent a friend a link to an article.

It was a piece about his company in the *Boston Business Journal*.

Was I marketing?

No, if you think marketing is "talking to hot prospects about business today."

Yes, if you think marketing is "staying in touch with the people you know, over and over again, in a way that positions you as a likeable expert."

Michael J. Katz

TODAY, I . . . spent half an hour after breakfast reading a business book.

I suppose I could have used that time to do "real work," but instead, I got two very good ideas from it.

If all you do every day is chase the work and do the work, you'll be doing the same thing ten years from now.

Make time to get better.

The Likeable Expert

TODAY, I . . . have lost nine newsletter subscribers.

. . . since I published my newsletter four days ago.

Does it mean I said something wrong or that they hate me or that I'm no longer relevant or . . . or . . . or??

I don't think so, since it happens every time.

Ignore the people that don't want to hear from you anymore (even the Beatles have ex-fans).

Cater to the ones that do.

Michael J. Katz

TODAY, I . . . called my own voice mail.

No, I wasn't checking up on myself.

I just wanted to see what it said, to make sure it was still on target.

I love automating aspects of my business, but if you don't check in on some of this stuff every once in a while, you may find it's no longer quite right.

The Likeable Expert

TODAY, I . . . went to see a doctor for a problem I've been having with my knee (don't ask).

I was impressed with how many questions he asked before diagnosing it, let alone suggesting treatment.

Where exactly does it hurt? How long have you had pain? Has the pain stayed the same over time? Does it hurt when I do this? How about this?

Effective selling works the same way.

We're all eager to offer our "proven solution." But before you do, try asking questions—lots and lots of them.

Not only does asking questions demonstrate an ability to listen (other humans like that), it reveals more about your expertise than does talking about yourself.

Michael J. Katz

TODAY, I . . . emailed a new client who was late in paying an invoice.

Not very late—just a day past thirty.

It's much easier, of course, to just do nothing and hope the check arrives eventually. And most times it does.

That said, if you're going to run a business, you need to get comfortable with the subject of money and learn to take quick action as necessary.

(She apologized for the delay and told me the check would go out tomorrow.)

The Likeable Expert

TODAY, I . . . had a guy come to the house to give us an estimate on new windows.

Wow, very expensive. When my wife and I flinched at the price he . . . did nothing.

He said their prices were firm and the same for everyone.

And you know what? I'm glad. Had he dropped the price based on our response, I would always wonder how low he would actually be willing to go.

By standing firm, he makes me feel that it's fair (even if we are priced out of hiring him).

When it comes to prospects saying yes—whether you sell windows or something else entirely—helping people believe they got a fair deal is as important as the price itself.

Michael J. Katz

TODAY, I . . . paid someone one day after receiving his invoice.

Sure, I could just sit on it for the customary thirty days. But for solo and small-business people, I find that we all get a pretty good sense of who the fast payers are and who the slow payers are.

I find that we fast payers get fast attention from the professionals we hire!

The Likeable Expert

TODAY, I . . . purchased the newly published book of a colleague, after running into him at a networking event.

I don't need the book. I don't even know if it's any good.

But you know how good it feels when someone "likes" something you posted on Facebook or LinkedIn? Having someone buy your book, on the spot, in cash, feels like that—multiplied by about a million!

Short money for helping make his day (and sometimes the books are really good).

Michael J. Katz

TODAY, I . . . had some work done on my car.

I like my mechanic but his estimates are always just a bit under the final bill. If he says $200, it's $225. If he says $450, it's going to be $500.

There's always a good reason ("sorry, forgot we had to flush the blah blah"), and I don't think it's deliberate at all. But even after all these years, there's always a little let down when they give me the bill.

I think it's better to work it the other way. Under-promising and over-delivering always feels better to the client.

The Likeable Expert

TODAY, I . . . took responsibility for a mistake I made with a client.

Not a big one (a slight delay in his newsletter publication), and I probably could have even said nothing.

Instead, I said sorry and said it was totally my fault (it was).

He said thanks, and it's over.

Always a little painful in the moment, but in the long run, I find these actually improve my relations with clients.

(Maybe I'll have to make some mistakes deliberately!)

Michael J. Katz

TODAY, I . . . listened to a radio program about dealing with addiction.

The phrase used regarding treatment was "progress not perfection."

Marketing (and running) a solo business is the same thing.

Do something—anything—to move your business forward every day.

Don't worry if it always seems like there's still more to do (there is).

The Likeable Expert

TODAY, I . . . spent twenty minutes on the phone with a woman who I knew would never hire me.

I knew because I could tell from her emails that I didn't want to work with her. She's too early in figuring out her business (she needs a life coach, not a marketing coach), and she's way (way) too intense and serious for me.

But I told her to give me a call and I'd offer any suggestions I could. We spoke for twenty minutes, at the end of which I suggested she find a coach.

But it wasn't a waste of my time either. I had twenty minutes to "be an expert." Twenty minutes to talk about what I do. Twenty minutes to help someone else

Spend time helping people. It always pays off.

Michael J. Katz

TODAY, I . . . added twenty-one new subscribers to my newsletter list.

I spoke at a business event last night and handed out a sheet of paper inviting people to sign up.

The exposure you get from speaking is nice, but it's a one-time event.

The real opportunity is getting permission to stay in touch—in some ongoing way—with people who like what you have to say.

The Likeable Expert

TODAY, I . . . received a call from a woman about speaking at an event in May.

I haven't seen her in person in eleven years (the last time she hired me to speak to her company).

Good thing I've kept in touch with her—through newsletters and the occasional email—all this time.

If you don't have (and use) a system for keeping relationships alive, you're working harder than you need to.

Michael J. Katz

TODAY, I . . . gently badgered a client who was trying to avoid my questions about how he was going to differentiate himself from his peers (other "management consultants").

It was a little uncomfortable at times since I wouldn't let it go and I thought I might be annoying him.

But in the end (two hours into it), we made great progress, and he apologized to me for "being difficult."

It's usually easier to not push so hard. But I find that if I just keep asking myself during those uncomfortable moments—"what's best for him?"—I'm able to stay with it, and the client is almost always happier at the end.

The Likeable Expert

TODAY, I . . . used my "lines I don't cross."

This is my personal list of things I don't do and/or require related to my work. One of them is a minimum fee for "getting on an airplane."

I love speaking to groups and in the past when someone would call and invite me to speak at a conference, it was hard for me to say no. So I came up with a rule: I need $xxx to get on an airplane . . . minimum.

Last week I was invited to speak at a conference, and they made me an offer on the speaker's fee. I told them my rule. I wasn't really negotiating. I just said I can't do it for less.

Interestingly, because I had already decided on it well before they called, it almost felt like it came from something bigger than just me. So it was easy for me to stand behind.

Five minutes ago they sent me an email agreeing to pay the fee.

What are your rules?

Michael J. Katz

TODAY, I . . . received an email from the place I bought my car with the subject line: "Customer Birthday."

It is, in fact, my birthday today. I commend whoever it is for devising a system for remembering anniversaries like this.

But Customer Birthday? As in, I assume, that well-known birthday classic "Customer Birthday to you."

Wait, it gets worse.

Inside the email, among other things, they told me that they "appreciate my patronage." Who am I, Benjamin Franklin?

Here's the point. Companies—even relatively small ones—can't get out of their own way when it comes to writing and speaking like normal humans.

As small-business owners, therefore, one of our key competitive advantages is to do otherwise.

The Likeable Expert

TODAY, I . . . ordered a book on Amazon for a client that I'll give to her the next time we meet.

It relates to some of the things we've been talking about, and I think she'll like it.

One of the benefits of charging clients a significant amount of money is that it gives you much more freedom for things like this.

I can easily justify spending $20 on a book—not nickel-and-diming people for little expenses, not worrying about how much time we spend together—because the overall fee is plenty high enough.

Interestingly, charging more money allows you to be more generous and less money focused in every other aspect of your work.

Michael J. Katz

TODAY, I . . . have a son turning 18.

I've also got a daughter who's 21 and another son who's 24.

In 2000, when I decided to start my own business, I didn't realize that (thanks to the flexibility of working solo) I was also deciding not to miss them growing up.

And I didn't.

When you run your own business, with all the worrying about finding clients, developing new services, paying the mortgage, etc., it's easy to forget how many great, often subtle things, are also part of the mix.

TODAY, I . . . am remembering.

The Likeable Expert

Michael J. Katz

About Michael J. Katz

An award-winning humorist and former corporate marketer, Blue Penguin founder and Chief Penguin, Michael Katz, specializes in helping professional service firms and solos get more and better clients by positioning themselves as Likeable Experts.

Since launching Blue Penguin in 2000, Michael has been quoted in *The Wall Street Journal, The New York Times,* Business Week Online, Bloomberg TV, Forbes.com, Inc.com, *USA Today*, and other national and local media.

He is the author of four books, and has published more than 400 issues of "The Likeable Expert Gazette," a twice-monthly email newsletter and podcast with 6,000 passionate subscribers in over 40 countries around the world.

Michael has an MBA from Boston University and a BA in Psychology from McGill University in Montreal. He also has a second degree black belt in karate, a first degree black belt in parenting (three children), and is a past winner of the New England Press Association award for "Best Humor Columnist."

Made in the USA
Lexington, KY
16 December 2017